"Know the Game" series

AMATEUR BOXING

Contents

	Page
Foreword	1
Amateur Boxing	2
Training	2
Gloves	3
Stance or Sparring Position	4
The Target	5
The Sport	6
Footwork	9
Attack	11
In-fighting	20
Defence	22
Down	28
Unfair Tactics	30
Seconds	34
Boxing Ring	35
Tactics	36
The "Southpaw"	38
Schools Amateur Boxing Association	40

Foreword

Interest in boxing has grown surprisingly during the past few years, particularly amongst boys in schools and clubs and we feel that the re-issue of this book is most opportune.

It is impossible to explain the whole art of boxing in a few pages, and it may well be said that there are as many methods of teaching as there are teachers, but this book certainly shows very clearly the correct actions and the faults to avoid. Anyone who studies the sketches herein and practises with determination and courage cannot fail to show considerable improvement.

The book has something for all—audience, seconds, would-be judges and referees, and last but not least, for the boxer himself. We have no hesitation in commending it to all interested in the Sport.

W. H. Young

Hon. General Secretary,
Schools Amateur Boxing Association.

AMATEUR BOXING

Boxing is a game. It must not be confused with fighting for there are certain well-defined rules which must be kept. It is a game of skill where two opponents equally matched, take part in a friendly attempt to outwit each other's boxing prowess. The sport calls for fitness of body and mind, and is the best way of obtaining those characteristics essential to all good citizens—confidence, reliance and control. Good habits, gentlemanly behaviour, cleanliness and neatness should be the aim of all.

In the boxing ring, particular attention must be given to the appearance.

TRAINING

Boxing requires stamina, agile bodies and minds— personal fitness is thus essential. Plenty of fresh air, regular hours, and simple exercises will help. P.E. instruction gives muscle strength to the arms, legs, back and stomach, while vaulting and other agility exercises give that necessary light freedom of movement. A punch pad improves speed and timing, while exercises on the punch bag ensures that blows are delivered with power.

Competitors should neither ask for nor accept embrocation, vaseline or other "aids" from any second. These are FORBIDDEN and are obnoxious to some competitors.

Note:
The official in charge has the right to prevent a boxer taking part in a contest if, in his opinion, the boxer's dress or appearance, for example length of hair, would be an impediment to the boxer or his opponent.

Appearance

Hair
Always well cut and carefully "parted"

Vest
A plain vest completely covering the chest and back, must be worn on every occasion.

Coloured Sash
Competitors must wear distinguishing colours, such as red or blue sashes round the waist, during a bout.

Shorts
These should be of reasonable length, reaching the mid-thigh position.

Footwear
Light gym shoes or boxing boots must be worn, with ankle socks which, if possible, should be white.

GLOVES

The "Knuckle Part"

Blows MUST land with the shaded part.

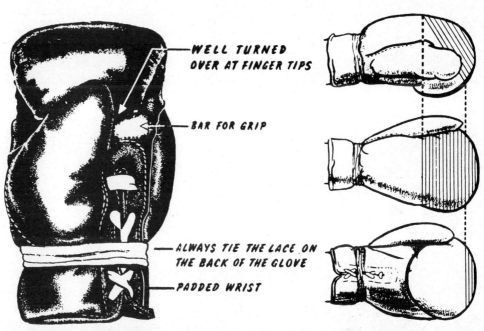

WELL TURNED OVER AT FINGER TIPS

BAR FOR GRIP

ALWAYS TIE THE LACE ON THE BACK OF THE GLOVE

PADDED WRIST

LONG, NARROW SHAPE

STANCE or SPARRING POSITION

Arms
Left elbow is bent, close in to the body, and behind the left glove which is held with the thumb uppermost.

Right glove is just below the chin with knuckle part toward opponent with right elbow tucked in.

Legs
Comfortably apart, with weight of body balanced evenly on both feet, left leg slightly bent.

Body
Left shoulder directed toward opponent: chin tucked in.

Feet
Left foot pointed in the direction of opponent; right heel raised. Left heel may be raised or ready to be raised; weight of body equally on the ball of each foot.

THE TARGET

Blows must land on the front or sides of the head or body above the belt. (This is an imaginary line drawn from the top of the hips through the navel.) Blows on the arms do not score.

Sketches in red show Illegal Blows

THE POINT

THE HEART

SOLAR PLEXUS "THE MARK"

Deliberate blows on the back of the neck

BLOWS DO NOT SCORE UNLESS ON THE TARGET

Hitting below the belt

The Kidney Punch

THE SPORT

Points are awarded for:

SCORING BLOWS—any fair blow delivered with the knuckle part of the closed glove of either hand contacting the target area with force.

All fair blows—successful "leads" or "counters" (i.e. whether delivered in attack or defence)—have the same scoring value.

ATTACK—may be successful or unsuccessful:

Successful: scoring blows delivered as "leads" (or blows struck first).

Unsuccessful: attempted "leads" that are blocked, warded off or evaded.

DEFENCE—all *evasive actions* such as ducking (illustrated on page 23), slipping (illustrated on page 24), weaving, guarding (the warding off, blocking or parrying of blows by arms or gloves) and

Getting away—A movement of the feet or body to avoid a blow.

A clean direct hit, used either in attack or defence, is a blow with the KNUCKLE part of the CLOSED glove of either hand on any part of the front or sides of the head or body above the belt.

The weight of the body must be behind the blow and the striker must not be infringing any of the rules when the blow is delivered.

It should be noted that the arms are not part of the target area.

Unfair Tactics

Hitting with open glove

No points are awarded for defensive actions, since defence earns its own reward by converting an attempted scoring blow into a non-scoring blow.

A *counter punch* is a defensive blow, not an attacking punch but is equal to a successful lead providing it conforms to the definition of a scoring blow.

Should the number of points awarded to the boxers be equal at the end of the bout, one additional point shall be awarded to the boxer who has shown the better defence.

Definitions: Scoring blows—See above.

Non-Scoring blows—Blows struck whilst committing any infringement of the rules. Blows on the arm or on the back. Soft blows or "taps" with no force behind them. Leading Off—Striking first, or attempting to strike first. Any infringement of the rules nullifies the scoring value of a leading off move.

Hitting with inside of glove

Hitting with butt of glove

Sketches in red show Unfair Tactics

Butting, or dangerous use of the head

Hitting with the elbow

Roughing

Shaking Hands

Boxers shake hands as illustrated. The "shake" should be made by firmly clasping each others gloves, and must not be a mere brush of the gloves.

A competitor will shake hands with his opponent twice only:

1. Immediately after the M.C. has announced both competitors. When the M.C. announces a competitor's name, the boy mentioned should stand to attention, facing the M.C. This will draw attention to his distinguishing colour.

2. Immediately after the result of the bout has been announced.

No other form of demonstration should take place at any time during a bout.

When the referee stops a bout to warn one of the contestants, the boxers do not shake hands when he gives the order to "Box on". When the decision is given, hand raising, shaking hands with seconds, jumping up and down, rushing across to an opponent to shake him by the hand, or patting him on the head, should have no place in amateur boxing.

FOOTWORK

Moving Forward

Advance the *left* foot *first*, followed by the right—just the same distance apart at the end of the movement as at the start.

Moving Back

The *right* foot is moved *first*, then the left foot. Both are gliding movements.

Moving to the right

Right foot moves first, followed by left.

TO RIGHT

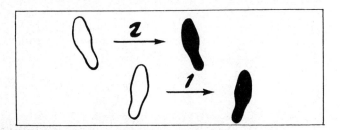

TO LEFT

Moving to the left

Left foot moves first, followed by right.

Moving round

Circle to your right, well up on the toes using small light, quick steps. This will keep you away from your opponent's right hand.

ATTACK

Alternative movement

Straight Left

Short step forward with left foot—at the same time straighten the left arm. Followed at once by bringing the right foot forward and so regaining sparring position.

When your opponent makes no move backward, then you must recover your original starting position, by bringing the left foot back following diagram 2.

Hook position of arm

Bend at hips to right

Left heel raised

Left Hook to Head

Boxers must be close together—blow can be delivered inside or over opponent's guard—bring left foot forward.

Elbow must be rigidly bent (like a "hook"); turn quickly at hip and down to the right toward opponent, raising *left* heel, and keeping the weight of the body on right foot.

Practise in front of a mirror (which shows the top half of the body) with right hooks, so that the action of a left hook can be seen.

If necessary turn the wrist to ensure that blow is struck with knuckle part.

Left Hook to Body

Similar punch as hook to head, except blow is aimed at front or side of body.

Right Hook to Body

Boxers must be fairly close together.

Make a definite twist round of the left shoulder to left side, slightly dropping it, and raise right heel well off the ground.

Right Hook to Head

A similar punch as hook to body except the arm is raised so that the blow lands on the head.

Practise in front of a mirror with left hooks and see the action of a right hook.

Right hand must be turned well over to land with the knuckle part.

Right Swing

Care must be taken to ensure that contact is made with the knuckle part of the glove. The right elbow is kept well raised and the right wrist turned outwards.

The Right Swing is a blow that should be sparingly used, since the action necessary for the correct delivery gives warning to an opponent, enabling him to use his left with advantage.

To avoid a right swing, sway slightly to the right and counter with a straight left.

A right swing can best be used to advantage against a Southpaw. As he leads, parry his right towards your right with the left and then lead with a right swing to head or body.

Just before delivery, the right arm is taken back and the body slightly turned to the right.

Left hand should be kept well up.

As the blow is made pivot sharply on the balls of both feet, adding force to the blow by turning to the left.

Short Swing

This blow can be used after stopping a left to the body (right arm guard) or a straight left to the head, by the open glove.

Lift the left shoulder

Knuckles should be held so that palm is turned outward

Left arm is almost straight and dropped to thigh

Step in with left foot, and swing left arm upwards and inwards

Uppercut

Uppercuts—with left or right hand—are useful damaging blows, but not easy to land. Damaged knuckles may result from incorrect delivery. They should be used sparingly.

Position of Feet
Immediately before the blow the right foot must be brought up almost level with the left.

Position of Arm
The punch must be delivered with the elbow bent, like a hook; glove being above the elbow.

Position of Hand
Palm of hand must be turned in towards body to hit with the large knuckles.

The uppercut can be used in ATTACK from the inside position.

Delivery of Blow

The right hip should turn quickly towards the opponent as the blow is delivered, raising right heel, and a lifting movement of shoulder to give weight to punch.

It can also be used in DEFENCE against an opponent who rushes in with head down and wild blows or as a counter to a left lead, by side stepping and uppercutting with left or right.

IN-FIGHTING

1. Aim at "getting in" close.

2. Head should be *near* your opponent's left shoulder.

3. Body blows are delivered slightly upwards and always with a swing of the shoulders.

4. Do not rush in—keep hands well up as guards.

INSIDE POSITION

To withdraw

1. Place gloves on opponent's arms, give a sharp push, and step back smartly

or

2. Press opponent's left arm from you with palm of right hand and side step to right, and away from his right hand.

Normal stance
It may be more comfortable and a better position for short arm punches to the body if the feet are in line.

The inside position for in-fighting may be obtained with:

1. **The outside parry**

    From a left lead, the right arm presses against the attacker's left forearm, so that the lead is forced outward and upward. Quickly step forward

    or

2. **A swinging blow**

    From this blow, you can easily get inside by putting up a guard, followed by a quick move forward, at the same time dropping the hands to commence hooking.

Cover for In-Fighting

Keep elbows well tucked into the sides, and hands ready to defend face or head; the body should be drawn back, and a slight crouch adopted.

To retreat safely, place the inside of the gloves on your opponent's biceps, giving him a sharp push away. Stand back quickly, keeping well covered.

DEFENCE

Using the open glove
Hold right hand well up, at the same time dropping the chin on the chest.

Using the arm
Throw right arm up with elbow nearly on a level with the shoulder to stop a left hook. Head should be lowered at the same time.

Using the Elbow
Drop left elbow firmly on body, at same time lowering the left shoulder.

Sketch in red shows a Foul

Swaying from a Straight Left

As the blow comes towards you, sway from the hips, bend slightly forward, to the right.

This is a form of defence which leaves both hands free and ready for a counter.

Snap Back

A sway backwards—a quick "snap" back from the hips, sufficient to be out of range of the blow.

Ducking

To duck to the right, lift the left heel and swing it outwards on the ball of the foot, at the same time bending the knees slightly—preserve the balance by letting the left arm drop backwards.

For ducking to the left the process is reversed.

Ducking is a simple way of avoiding a right swing. Do no more than let the blow just miss, for if too deep, i.e. ducking below the "belt", it is a foul.

Slipping   # Counter Hitting

A short step forward and sideways with either the left or the right foot according to your opponent's blow; this leaves both hands free for an attack.

Slipping a Right
A short step forward and sideways leaving opponent open to a right.

Slipping a Straight Left and Countering with Right
A quick swerve round on balls of feet after side stepping.

Left Hand Counter to a Straight Right
On a right lead, step well in with the left foot, and counter with a left hook over opponent's extended right arm.

Right Hand Cross Counter
Draw left lead—send in a hard right over opponent's left arm, stepping well in with left foot and swerve to left.

Left Hand Hook to Body
Step in with left foot.

Right Hand Hook to Body
Step well in keeping elbow as close to the side as possible.

Side Stepping

To get out of the way of an opponent who rushes in, move the right foot first, forwards and sideways to come level with your left, and with a quick twist on the ball of the foot, followed by placing the left foot in its correct position, you are ready to attack.

Inside Parry

The body is swayed slightly to the right, and the right hand presses the attacker's left forearm to the left, leaving him open for a counter blow.

Cross Guards

Give the oncoming left a smart tap near the wrist with the left hand; keep the chin well in, and the left elbow fairly high.

The Break

When contestants' arms become linked in a clinch, the Referee's order of "Break" must be immediately acted upon, by each competitor stepping back a pace before commencing boxing. The "Break" must be clean and decisive.

Hitting on the "break" is against the rules.

DOWN

A boxer is considered to be "down" when any part of his body other than his feet is touching the ground, or if he is outside the ropes, or partly outside the ropes, or hangs helplessly on the ropes.

Whenever the line of the ring is broken, a boxer is said to be "down".

The Count

Under Schools A.B.A. Rules there is no "count" by the Referee when a boxer is "Down".

The timekeeper shall keep a silent record of the passing seconds and will indicate to the Referee when the Boxer has been down for ten seconds—**unless the Referee has not previously stopped the bout.** (Under A.B.A. Rules the timekeeper indicates to the referee the passing seconds, by an arm movement, and the referee synchronises a similar arm movement as a visual indication to the boxer who is "down".)

One knee down

Both hands on floor

Arm through ropes

Lying on ropes

Partly through the ropes

Through the ropes

Boxer Stands Back

When a boxer is "down", his opponent must immediately retire to the farther neutral corner where he shall remain until ordered to resume boxing by the Referee. Whether the Referee gives the warning "Stand Back" or not, boxing must not recommence until the order "Box on".

If at the end of a round, other than the last round of a bout, a competitor is "down", the gong indicating the end of a round will not be sounded. The gong will be sounded only when the Referee gives the command "Box", indicating the continuation of the round.

Sketch in red shows a Foul

Pivot blow

Semi-pivot blow

Lying-on

Sketches in red show Unfair Tactics

UNFAIR TACTICS

The following are not permitted:

Pivot Blow
Delivered by swinging round in a complete circle.

Semi-Pivot Blow
The boxer having missed with the swinging blow, comes back with the forearm striking with a back handed blow.

"Lying-on"
If a boxer's head or body is pressing against an opponent, he is said to be "lying-on".

"Lying-on" with head or body is the resort of the inferior boxer to avoid being hit or to obtain an unfair advantage.

No credit is given for any blows struck when "lying-on".

Sketches in red show Unfair Tactics

Holding and Hitting
Deliberately obstructing a boxer's movements by trapping or gripping his arm, or by holding him round the waist spoils good boxing.

No judge will give any credit for correct blows—such as this upper-cut—given while committing a foul.

Sketches in red show Unfair Tactics

Shouldering
May occur through a thoughtless attack, such as rushing in with the head down.

Wrestling
Any attempt to throw the other boxer is regarded as being unfair tactics.

Covering-Up
A boxer must *not* persistently cover-up. He *can* cover up to avoid an unexpected attack or to get out of an awkward position.

The ropes are provided to keep the boxers within the confined space of the "ring".

Pretending to fall or slip down, is the poor boxer's way of avoiding an expected blow.

This and other unsportsmanlike actions are entirely out of place in amateur boxing.

For all fouls the referee has the power to disqualify a boxer.

Sketches in red show Unfair Tactics

Using the rope as a lever to gain impetus for a blow is not permitted.

A boxer makes an unfair use of the ropes when he holds the rope with one hand and hits his opponent with the other.

SECONDS

A boxer is allowed two seconds, one who attends to him personally, and an assistant who is not permitted to enter the ring but will have available whatever the official second requires.

A second should look neat in appearance and be dressed in accordance with the rules. He should be calm and efficient, and ready to offer cheerful advice should it be needed.

Duties of a Second

1. Escort his competitor to the appropriate corner of the ring.
2. Advise his competitor only during the interval of each round.
3. See that his charge is relaxed as far as possible during the minute rest—wipe his face, moisten his mouth and generally see that he is ready for the next round.

The following practices should be discouraged as being useless to a fit competitor:

1. Flapping the towel during the minute rest.

Flapping of a towel will not assist a competitor to recover any sooner, nor will a second who stands over and "crowds" him help in any way. Many competitors have put up with, and accepted, this treatment, much against their inclinations.

2. Massage of the body.

In general, massage of the abdomen, etc., has no place in the boxing ring.
3. The use of embrocation, vaseline or any stimulant other than water is strictly forbidden.

BOXING RING

The measurements of the ring should be not less than 12 feet (3.65 m) or more than 16 feet (4.87 m) square. The height from ring floor level to the top rope should be not less than four feet (1.20 m) or more than five feet (1.50 m). The ring should be formed by at least two sets of ropes (preferably three) and the ropes covered with linen or similar soft material. The platform should be safely constructed, level and free from any obstructing projections and should extend for at least 15 inches (37.5 cm) outside the line of the ropes.

It should be fitted with four corner posts which should be well padded or otherwise so constructed to prevent injury to the boxers. The floor should be covered with a rubber underlay, over which canvas should be stretched and secured in place.

The underlay and canvas should cover the entire platform.

While a bout is in progress the platform must be cleared of all chairs, buckets, etc.

Corner of the Ring

Requirements

1. Stool.
2. Bucket of cool, clean water.
3. Personal beaker.
4. Sponge and towel.
5. Bowl of sawdust.
6. Box of resin.

TACTICS

Getting Out of a Corner

1. Push opponent's left arm with right, just above elbow—turn him round—step forward with right foot, slipping along the ropes.

2. A side stepping movement can also be used to get out of a corner.

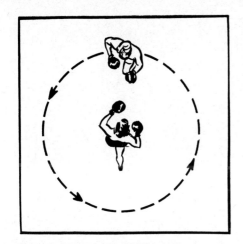

Dominating the Ring

Keeping to the centre of the ring, making your opponent do all the work of circling and weaving, causing him to tire, thus slowing his punching and footwork, and making him careless in defence.

Feinting

Used to confuse an opponent. If, for instance, your opponent is vulnerable to a left to the head, open his defence with a feint to the head, and immediately follow with a left to the body.

To avoid a right swing, sway slightly to the right and counter with a straight left.

THE SOUTHPAW

A boxer who stands with his right arm extended is known as a "Southpaw". A looking glass reflection of the conventional type. His advantage is that he usually meets the orthodox boxer, while the orthodox boxer seldom meets the "Southpaw".

There should be occasional practice against such a boxer, remembering:

1. You must now move to the left.
2. The most successful blow to use is a right hook to the head or body, swerving to the left as the right hand is led to you, before countering.
3. If you wish to attempt a long left hook, do not forget to put up your right hand guard.
4. Be wary of his strong left hand.

Footwork. Never move to his left hand.

Coax him to lead

If he leads with a "straight right" use your right hand for an outside parry, swerving to the left to keep outside of the lead.

He is then open for a long over arm hook to the chin.

Parrying with the left hand

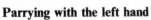

Outwards. Step in, simultaneously connecting your right with his head or body before he can bring over his left.

or *Inwards* (as illustrated). This is the safer method to adopt.

Push his lead to your right, leaving an opening for your right hand. You are for a moment so placed that you cannot be hit.

A right swing can best be used to advantage against a Southpaw. As he leads, parry his right towards your right with your left, and then lead with a right swing to head or body.

SCHOOLS AMATEUR BOXING ASSOCIATION

The objects of the Schools Amateur Boxing Association are:

The advancement of boxing among schoolboys
All schools are eligible to affiliate through county associations, or where there is no county association, by direct affiliation.

Guidance upon methods of teaching and judging
Courses for Instructors, Judges and Referees are regularly held throughout the country, wherever there is the demand. Examinations, both oral and practical are arranged for purposes of qualification.

The conduct of Competitions
Conditions for tournaments are constantly under review to ensure that there is no undue physical or mental strain for the schoolboy boxer.

The improvement and extension of facilities for boxing in schools
With the co-operation of those responsible for the organisation of Physical Education in schools, advice is given on the purchase of suitable equipment, and the inclusion of the sport in the normal school curriculum.

Further information or advice may be obtained from:
The Hon. General Secretary, W. H. Young,
16 Curtis Road, Hounslow, Middlesex, TW4 5PT.
Telephone No: 01-894 5856

Printed in Great Britain by John Blackburn Ltd., Leeds 10